Amazing
Journeys

Written by Margaret Clyne
and Rachel Griffiths

sundance™

Contents

Introduction

Many animals make long and difficult journeys to find food or places for their young to start life. They often travel great distances, sometimes even halfway around the world.

Some animals make one of these amazing journeys every year; others make only one amazing journey in their lives.

Some animals travel over land, some travel through water, and some travel in the air.

Before winter starts, these geese set off on a journey to feeding grounds. They return the following summer.

Journeys over Land

Caribou

Caribou are a type of reindeer that live in North America. During summer, caribou feed on the grass and leaves of the **tundra**, the treeless plains near the **Arctic Circle**.

As winter approaches, food becomes harder to find. Small herds of caribou join together to form a huge herd. Thousands and thousands of caribou travel south to the forests where food can be found.

Journeys over Land

Emperor penguins begin the long journey over land before winter begins.

Emperor Penguins

Emperor penguins live in the waters near **Antarctica**. They can swim very well, but they cannot fly, and they find it difficult to walk.

8

Once a year, the penguins make an amazing journey over land to their **nesting colony**. On the journey, they slide over the ice on their stomachs and push themselves with their flippers.

As summer begins, the young chicks are almost ready to make the journey to the sea.

Journeys Through Water

Green Turtles

Green turtles spend most of their lives at sea, but they come ashore to lay their eggs. Every few years, full-grown female turtles swim long distances to the beach where they were hatched. This is where they lay their eggs.

Some turtles may travel over 1,240 miles (2,000 kilometers) to reach the same beach.

No one knows for sure how these turtles find the same beach again.

The male green turtle spends all of his life in the sea. Only the female swims to the shore to lay her eggs.

Journeys Through Water

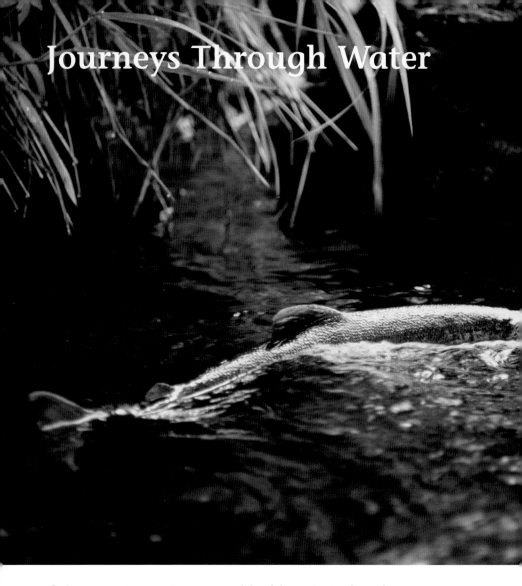

Salmon swim upstream and build nests to lay their eggs in.

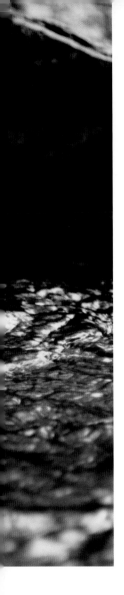

Salmon

Salmon live most of their lives in the sea. But they leave the sea and battle their way up freshwater streams to lay their eggs.

Young salmon hatch from eggs buried in gravel nests that their parents built. After a little while, the young salmon return to the sea where they grow into adult salmon.

Four or five years later, the adult salmon return to the same streams to lay their eggs.

Some salmon swim up **rapids** and waterfalls to reach their breeding grounds. Salmon make this amazing journey without eating.

Journeys in the Air

Monarch Butterflies

Monarch butterflies live in the United States and Canada. At the end of summer, they fly south to Mexico.

In spring, they fly back north. During this journey, the adults lay their eggs, and then they die. When the young butterflies hatch, they continue the journey north.

These butterflies are tiny, but fly an enormous distance on fragile wings. Their wings are often tattered by the end of their amazing journey. No one knows exactly how the young butterflies know where to go.

Journeys in the Air

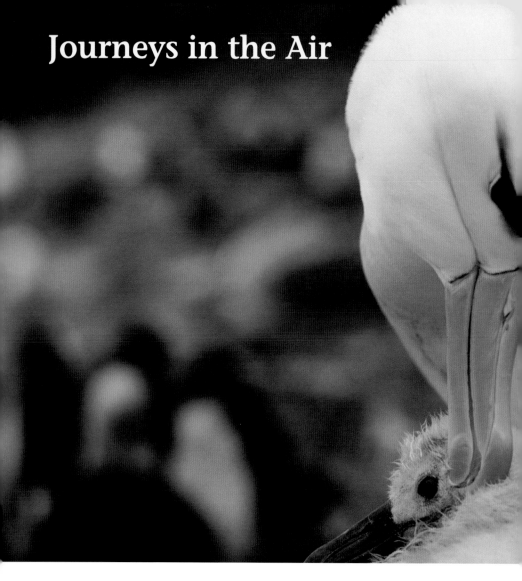

A black-browed albatross with its young.

Albatross

Albatross spend most of their lives gliding over the sea in search of food. They swoop down to catch fish and squid from the sea.

Albatross travel great distances without ever seeing land or landing. They are able to sleep while they are gliding in the air.

Albatross come to land to nest and lay their eggs. They stay ashore to look after their young.

Conclusion

Many animals make amazing journeys. Their journeys are often long, difficult, and dangerous.

The journeys that the animals take are full of risks, but they help the animals to survive.

Humpback whales feed in polar regions in the summer. As winter approaches, they travel long distances to the warm tropical oceans to give birth to their young.

Glossary

Antarctica	the frozen continent in the southern polar region
Arctic Circle	the boundary of the northern polar region
nesting colony	a large group of animals that gather together to look after their young
rapids	a part of a river where the current is very strong and fast
tundra	treeless plains near the Arctic Circle